NAILED IT!

Extreme

BMX
FREESTYLE

Virginia Loh-Hagan

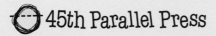
45th Parallel Press

Published in the United States of America by Cherry Lake Publishing
Ann Arbor, Michigan
www.cherrylakepublishing.com

Content Adviser: Liv Williams, Editor, www.iLivExtreme.com
Reading Adviser: Marla Conn, ReadAbility, Inc.
Photo Credits: ©ASchindl/Shutterstock.com, cover, 1; ©Haslam Photography/Shutterstock.com, 5; ©A.Ricardo/Shutterstock.com, 6; ©Bigben0123/Dreamstime.com, 9; ©Dmitryelagin/Dreamstime.com, 11; ©Homydesign/Shutterstock.com, 12; ©Smileimage9/Shutterstock.com, 15; ©Dmitryelagin/Dreamstime.com, 17; ©Steve Boyle/ZUMAPRESS/Newscom, 19; ©Phillipgray/Dreamstime.com, 21; ©Lilyana Vynogradova/Shutterstock.com, 23; ©Majimus/Dreamstime.com, 25; ©Pkripper503/Dreamstime.com, 26; ©Suzanne Tucker/Shutterstock.com, 29; ©Trusjom/Shutterstock.com, multiple interior pages; ©Kues/Shutterstock.com, multiple interior pages

Copyright © 2016 by Cherry Lake Publishing
All rights reserved. No part of this book may be reproduced or utilized in any
form or by any means without written permission from the publisher.

45th Parallel Press is an imprint of Cherry Lake Publishing.

Library of Congress Cataloging-in-Publication Data

Loh-Hagan, Virginia.
  Extreme BMX freestyle / Virginia Loh-Hagan.
     pages cm. -- (Nailed It!)
  Includes bibliographical references and index.
  ISBN 978-1-63470-016-0 (hardcover) -- ISBN 978-1-63470-070-2 (pdf) -- ISBN 978-1-63470-043-6 (paperback) -- ISBN 978-1-63470-097-9 (ebook)
  1. BMX freestyle (Stunt cycling)--Juvenile literature. 2. Extreme sports--Juvenile literature. 3. ESPN X-Games--Juvenile literature. 4. Extreme BMX freestyle. I. Title.

  GV1049.3.L65 2015
  796.04'6--dc23

                    2015006300

ABOUT THE AUTHOR

Dr. Virginia Loh-Hagan is an author, university professor, former classroom teacher, and curriculum designer. She is one of the few people who have forgotten how to ride a bike. She lives in San Diego with her very tall husband and very naughty dogs. To learn more about her, visit www.virginialoh.com.

Table of Contents

No Excuses!

Who is Kevin Robinson? Who is Colton Satterfield? Why are they good examples of extreme BMX freestyle riders?

Kevin Robinson is riding his BMX bike. He speeds up the **half-pipe**. The half-pipe is a U-shaped ramp. He spins upside down. He crashes. He is trying to **land**, or complete, the double flair. The double flair is a trick. It's two backflips while spinning in the air.

Robinson keeps trying. He said, "I just want to pull a double flair … I don't care if it's midnight and the lights are off and everybody is gone." He keeps crashing. He keeps trying.

Robinson finally makes BMX history. He is the first to land the double flair. He said, "This was three years in the making … It's that moment of accomplishing something that you've never done before." For three years, he's been practicing this trick. He didn't quit.

Kevin Robinson competes in the X Games. It is a competition for extreme sports.

Robinson set another record. He got the highest **air** on his BMX bike. Getting air means getting high in the air. He rode up a giant **quarterpipe**. A quarterpipe is half of a U-shaped ramp. He was 27 feet (8.2 meters) above the ramp.

Robinson makes no excuses. He has broken about 25 bones. He's had at least 50 blows to the head. He's had 45 surgeries. Nothing stops him.

The MegaRamp consists of the roll-in ramp, the gap jump, and the final quarterpipe ramp.

6m

5m

4m

3m

Voice from the Field: Aaron Fotheringham

Aaron Fotheringham definitely makes no excuses. He lost the use of his legs. He had a condition. But that didn't stop him from being a BMXer. He said, "When I was a little kid, I was always watching X Games with my older brother. And he was a BMXer." Fotheringham went with his brother to the skateboard park. His brother told him to try it on his wheelchair. Fotheringham did. He fell on his face. He didn't quit. He practices what he calls "hardcore sitting." He does crazy tricks on his wheelchair. He uses moves from BMX free riding and skateboarding. He said, "I'm so pumped to be able to get out there and show people what a wheelchair can do. That it doesn't hold you back." He has a special wheelchair. He set a world record. He did the first complete backflip in a wheelchair. Watch videos of Aaron's stunts on his website: http://aaronfotheringham.com.

Robinson tried to do a backflip on the **MegaRamp**. The MegaRamp is a really huge ramp. He missed. He crashed to the bottom. He was knocked out. But he kept trying. He said, "I don't have the capability of backing off." Extreme BMX freestyle stars like Robinson don't know how to quit.

Colton Satterfield tore his knee. He broke his tailbone. He broke his wrist. He also cracked his skull. Nothing stopped him from BMX riding.

He likes landing big new tricks. He rode his BMX bike down the MegaRamp. He jumped across a big gap. He flew 30 feet (9 m) into the air. He took his hands off the **handlebars**. Handlebars are the steering bars on a bike. Satterfield did a circle spin in the air. He grabbed his handlebars. He spun them around. He did this while doing a backflip. This trick had never been done before.

Extreme BMX riders are always inventing new challenges.

"Extreme BMX freestyle stars like Robinson don't know how to quit."

Extreme BMX freestyle riders like to do tricks in the air.

Going Off Track

How did BMX riding start? Who is Bob Haro? What is BMX freestyle riding? How did BMX freestyle riders copy skateboarders?

BMX stands for bicycle **motorcross**. Motorcross is when riders race motorcycles around dirt tracks. Motorcross riders make sharp turns. They jump over steep hills.

BMX riding started in the 1960s. It started in Southern California. Dirt tracks were tough on the riders' bikes. They would land hard on their bikes. Bikes bent. Wheels broke. Tires got flattened.

The kids needed better bikes. Bikes needed to be closer to the ground. This made them stronger. Kids **souped up** their bikes. They changed bikes to fit their needs.

BMX bikes turn quickly. They handle jumps easily. They have small wheels. The tires have **knobbies**, or bumps. The knobbies grip the dirt. There's a hand brake to stop and slow the bike. There are also **pegs**. Pegs are rods on the side of the bike. Riders stand on the pegs. They stand to do tricks.

BMX racing was popular. The goal was to be the fastest

BMX bikes have to be strong and light so that the riders can do tricks.

rider. But some kids wanted more. They wanted to do tricks off the tracks.

In the late 1970s, BMX riding changed. Bob Haro landed the first "rock walk." A rock walk is a trick. BMX freestyle riding was born. It's more about doing tricks than racing.

Kids invented this sport. They didn't stick to the rules. They copied skateboarders. They rode in skate parks. They rode in empty swimming pools. They popped **wheelies**. Wheelies are when the front wheel is off the ground. They stood on their bike seats.

BMX riders show off. They like to outperform each other.

Extreme BMX Freestyle: Know the Lingo

Amped: excited

Bail: pulling out of a trick to avoid wiping out

Corndog: rider who gets dirty

Fakie: riding backward

Gnarly: beyond rad, beyond extreme, perfection; dangerous

Hot shoe: putting a foot on the ground to help balance

Huck: throwing yourself into a trick

Kickout: throwing the bike to the side in midair

Nothing: taking both hands and feet off the bike

Pogoing: hopping on one tire

Potato chip: wheel that gets bent

Rad: cool, radical

Road rash: long, painful scrapes caused by wiping out

Roller: single jump on a hill

Shred: hard, fast riding

Sidewalking: hopping sideways

Step up: one small jump followed by a larger one

Whoop-de-dos: series of small hills

Wired: doing a trick correctly

There's a Style for Every Rider!

What are the different types of BMX freestyle riding? What is an example of each type of BMX freestyle riding?

There are many types of BMX freestyle riding. There are no rules in stunt riding. The riders do whatever they want. They just have to be creative and safe.

Flatland riding is when riders do tricks on smooth ground. Riders ride in parking lots. They also ride in basketball courts. Riders flip bikes into strange positions. Riders spin and balance on one wheel. They can touch anything on their bikes. But they can't touch the ground. They can't stop riding until their routines are done.

Matthias Dandois is a BMX flatlander. He's always moving. He looks like he's break dancing on his bike.

Street riding is the most popular form of BMX freestyle. Street riders use city streets and **obstacles**. Obstacles are

BMX flatland riders look like they're dancing.

things riders use to get air. They do tricks on curbs. They do tricks on stairs. They do tricks on benches. They **grind**, or slide. They jump. They often don't use brakes.

Garrett Reynolds won seven X Games gold medals for

When Extreme Is Too Extreme!

Rick Thorne is a professional BMX rider. He began riding at 12 years old. He did a "wall ride" on a moving semi-truck. A wall ride is a trick. The rider rides on a wall. Thorne rode on a moving wall. He gained speed. He went toward the wall, or side of the truck. He pulled up his front tire. He did a small hopping motion. He rode the wall. He kept pedaling. He leaned out so that he could come down. A wall rider is a basic trick. But Thorne made it hard by doing it on a moving truck. He also set himself on fire. Then he rode a full pipe. He's extreme!

BMX street riders do spins and flips on street obstacles.

street riding. He said, "Street riding is so much about using your muscles to pull and pop tricks."

Reynolds and some friends fixed a railing in Delaware. They wanted to ride it. But they also wanted to save it for other riders. It's important to leave obstacles in good shape.

Dirt riding is also called trail riding. It's when riders ride dirt trails. The trails have small dirt hills or bumps. They jump over these bumps. They do as many tricks as they can. They also build their own jumps.

Riders create two dirt bumps. One is the **lip**. A lip is a steep takeoff. It helps riders get speed and air. The second bump is the landing. It is less steep and wider. The area between the bumps is called the gap. Dirt riders focus on doing tricks in the air.

Corey Bohan won many BMX dirt awards. He does backflips at over 20 feet (6 m) in the air. He is known for going high. He also combines several tricks.

Park riding is when riders do tricks in skateboard parks. Park riders are similar to skateboarders. They ride up curved ramps. They jump over boxes. They do tricks in the air.

Dennis Enarson started as a BMX racer. He changed to park riding at 8 years old. He thought it was more fun. He designed his own BMX course. He combines tricks. He moves from ramp to ramp.

"Dirt riders focus on doing tricks in the air."

Corey Bohan has been voted "Dirt Jumper of the Year" several times.

Julien Dupont rode his bike in a roller coaster park. He rode on a wooden roller coaster. It was in Mexico. It was about 1 mile (1.6 kilometers) long. He was 110 feet (33.5 m) above ground. He did wheelies and backflips on the tracks. He said, "It was the sickest ride ever!"

Vertical riding is when riders speed up big ramps. They also speed up pipes. They launch into the air. They do tricks. Their goal is to get vertical. They want to get straight up into the air.

Mat Hoffman is a famous BMX vertical rider. He does many daring stunts. He rode his bike off a cliff in Norway. The cliff is 3,200 feet (975 m) above ground. He did two backflips. Then he glided down to the ground. He used a **parachute**. A parachute looks like a balloon top. It slowed him down as he landed. He also rode his bike out of an airplane. He was 16,000 feet (4,877 m) above ground.

"It was the sickest ride ever!"

Skateboard parks have bowls, boxes, and ramps.

Hoffman won a gold medal with three broken bones in his foot. He is known as "The Condor." A condor is a large bird. Hoffman looks like he's flying. He's the first person to complete a no-handed 900. A 900 is two and a half spins in the air.

Vertical riding is also called vert riding.

Falling and Getting Up!

What are different words for falling? Why is falling important to extreme BMX riding? Who is Dave Mirra?

Extreme BMX riders push limits. Freestyling is about creativity and courage. Riders are always improving moves. They add their own twists to classic stunts. Riders spend hours practicing. They spend hours healing. They fall a lot.

Falling is a big part of extreme BMX freestyle riding. Riders have many words for falling. They include: munch, crash and burn, beater, biff, chunder, wipe out, and zonk.

Dave Mirra knows all about falling and getting up. He was

hit by a drunk driver. He was crossing the street. It almost killed him. He hurt his shoulder. He cracked his skull. He got blood **clots**, or lumps, in his brain. Doctors told him he couldn't ride again. Mirra didn't let that stop him.

It took him six months to heal. He got back on his bike. He won several gold medals. He said, "It was a setback, but something I overcame. It doesn't even mess with me at all.

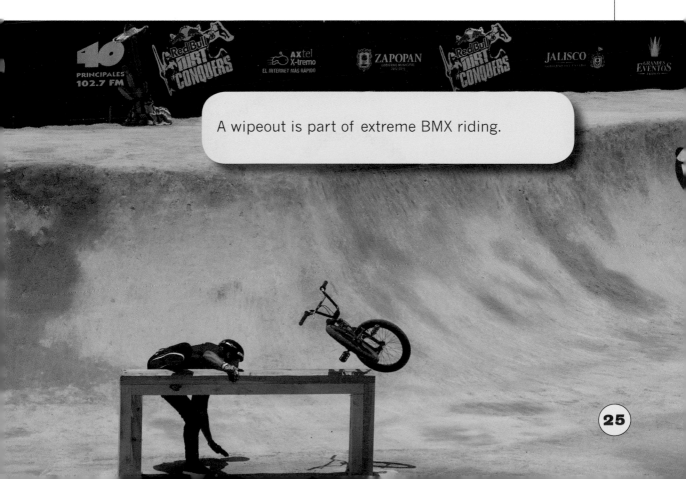

A wipeout is part of extreme BMX riding.

In life there are obstacles you have to go through. Whatever it is, you overcome it eventually."

Mirra invented his own stunts. His nickname is "Miracle Man." He did a double backflip. This is a hard trick. Both rider and bike do two backflips in the air.

Mirra always wanted to be a BMX rider. He started when he was young. He and his friends practiced riding a lot.

A BMX magazine voted Dave Mirra "Freestyler of the Year."

Spotlight Biography: Natalie Wade

There aren't many professional female BMX riders. Natalie Wade is a female BMX freestyler. She mostly rides in skateboard parks. But she also loves jumping from a good vertical ramp. Natalie competes in the contests that allow females. Some of these contests are: Ray's, JoMoPro, Toronto BMX Jam, and BMX Masters. She's married to Morgan Wade. He is another BMX freestyler. He is known for his big stunts. Morgan and Natalie included BMX riding in their wedding. They rode away from their party on a tandem bike. A tandem bike is a bike made for two people. Natalie is making a movie about four BMX female riders. The title is *Chick Flick*. It will be the first all-girl BMX video.

They challenged and encouraged each another. He was dedicated to the sport. He said, "Anything you want to get better at is a commitment. Without commitment, there would be no success."

Extreme BMX riders don't let anything get in their way.

"Anything you want to get better at is a commitment. Without commitment, there would be no success."

A good BMX freestyler needs to practice a lot.

Did You Know?

- Matthias Dandois is a BMX world champion. Sam Partaix is a professional BMX rider. They jumped in a water-filled swimming pool. They were at a private castle in France. They did tricks underwater. They performed all kinds of tricks on their bikes.

- BMX tricks are given names. They are usually named by the inventors. For example, Bill Nitschke landed a trick in a Burger King parking lot. He named the trick "Whopper." It is also known as a "bunnyhop tailwhip." It is a flatland trick.

- Bob Haro performed most of the BMX stunts in Steven Spielberg's movie *E.T. the Extra-Terrestrial*.

- Extreme BMX freestyle riders have their own language. Try to understand this: "He got a nothing to rail done. He also nothing'ed down the stairs and did a nose wheelie to footjam over the volcano."

- Corey Bohan is a BMX dirt rider. He is probably more famous for being Audrina Patridge's ex-boyfriend. Patridge starred in the popular reality show called *The Hills*.

- Some BMX riders refer to their bikes as "little kids' bikes."

Consider This!

TAKE A POSITION! Female BMX riders have a hard time getting sponsorships. This means they have a hard time competing in contests. Simple Session is a contest. In 2012, Estonia hosted a Simple Session contest. It was the first time a major contest allowed women to compete with men. Do you think women should be allowed to compete in BMX freestyle competitions? Argue your position with reasons and evidence.

SAY WHAT? Learn more about BMX racing. Explain how BMX freestyle is different from BMX racing.

THINK ABOUT IT! Kids riding bikes in a concrete structure started BMX riding. Extreme sports like BMX riding and skateboarding were created by kids for kids. What sport would you like to invent?

SEE A DIFFERENT SIDE! Skateboarders created skate parks because they were banned from skating on streets and city parks. Now, some skateboarders are banning BMX riders from riding in their parks. They are afraid of crashes. The bikes also ruin the surface of the skate parks. How do you think skateboarders feel about BMX riders?

Learn More: Resources

PRIMARY SOURCES

A Day in the Life of BMX Rider Kevin Robinson, www.abullseyeview.com/2012/04/day-in-the-life-of-bmx-rider-kevin-robinson/

Hoffman, Mat. *The Ride of My Life*. New York: Harper Entertainment, 2002.

SECONDARY SOURCES

Bishop, Amanda, and Bobbie Kalman. *Extreme BMX*. New York: Crabtree Publishing Company, 2004.

Doeden, Matt. *BMX Freestyle*. Mankato, MN: Capstone Press, 2005.

Sandler, Michael. *Daring BMXers*. New York: Bearport Publishing, 2010.

WEB SITES

American Bicycle Association: http://usabmx.com

International BMX Freestyle Federation: X Games—BMX: http://www.ibmxff.org/

Glossary

air (AIR) jumping, being high in the air

clots (KLOTS) lumps of blood

grind (GRINDE) slide bike on an obstacle

half-pipe (HAF-pipe) a U-shaped ramp

handlebars (HAN-duhl-bahrz) steering bars on a bike

land (LAND) complete or accomplish

lip (LIP) steep jump or ramp used to take off or launch into the air

knobbies (NOB-eez) bumps or grooves in the tire, used to grip dirt

MegaRamp (MEG-uh-ramp) a really large skate structure used for big air contests

motorcross (MOH-tuh-kraws) motorcycle riders riding in dirt tracks

obstacles (OB-stuh-kuhlz) things riders use to get air

parachute (PAR-uh-shoot) strong, light fabric attached to thin ropes that helps jumpers slow down their fall

pegs (PEGZ) rods on the side of the bike

quarterpipe (KWOR-tuhr-pipe) half of a U-shaped ramp

souped up (SOOPD UP) customized or changed to fit your needs

vertical (VUR-ti-kuhl) straight up in the air

wheelies (WHEEL-eez) tricks where the front wheel is off the ground

Index